A COLORADO AUTUMN

Photography by John Fielder

Foreword by Jim Carrier

WESTCLIFFE PUBLISHERS, INC., ENGLEWOOD, COLORADO

ACKNOWLEDGMENTS

I dedicate this book to a person whose teaching influenced me to ultimately make a career related to nature. Dolly Hickman was my science teacher for several years in junior high school in my home town of Charlotte, North Carolina. Mrs. Hickman's personal love of science and nature, her ability to guide sometimes disoriented adolescent minds, and her passion for fostering a fascination for all things natural affected many students during her long career. I, for one, am grateful to her for planting a seed of "curiosity" in my mind during formative years. In large part, that planting is the reason why I do what I do today.

— J.F.

Selected quotations reprinted with permission from the following:

A Clearing in the Wilderness, by Hugh Fosburgh.
Bantam Doubleday Dell, New York, 1969.

A Walk Through the Year, by Edwin Way Teale.
Dodd, Mead & Company, New York, 1978.

America the Beautiful, In the Words of Henry David Thoreau,
by the editors of "Country Beautiful." Country Beautiful Corporation,
Waukesha, Wisconsin, 1966.

Great Wilderness Days, In the Words of John Burroughs,
by the editors of "Country Beautiful." Country Beautiful Corporation,
Waukesha, Wisconsin, 1975.

Homeland, A Report from the Country, by Hal Borland.
J.B. Lippincott Company, Philadelphia, 1969.

John Burroughs' America, edited by Farida A. Wiley.
The Devin-Adair Company, New York, 1951.

Journeys in Green Places, by Virginia S. Eifert.
Dodd, Mead & Company, New York, 1963.

The Autumn Book, edited by James Reeves.
Heinemann, London, 1977.

The Last Beautiful Days of Autumn, by John Nichols.
Holt Rinehart and Winston, New York, 1982.

This Hill, This Valley, by Hal Borland.
Simon and Schuster, New York, 1957.

International Standard Book Number: 1-56579-083-9
Library of Congress Catalog Number: 94-060590
Copyright © John Fielder, 1994. All rights reserved.
Published by Westcliffe Publishers, 2650 South Zuni Street, Englewood, Colorado 80110
Publisher, John Fielder; Editor, Ann Higman; Designer, Leslie Gerarden
Printed in Singapore by Tien Wah Press

First Frontispiece: *Sunrise, Gunnison National Forest, along East Muddy Creek*
Second Frontispiece: *The Dyke stands behind aspen groves along the Kebler Pass road, near Crested Butte*
Third Frontispiece: *First snow, Weston Pass road, near Fairplay*
Title Page: *Narrow leaf cottonwoods along the Dolores River, near Dolores*
Opposite: *Pine and scrub oak, Castle Pines, near Denver*

FOREWORD

There is nothing so sweet or sad as a country road in autumn. Nothing that invites us more to enter into beauty. Nothing else tugs so strongly at life that is temporal.

I think of fall as the season of movement: man, animal, leaves and sun, birds, snowbirds — all of us on some road. The rancher pushes cattle down from higher pastures. The farmer harvests before the frost. Elk and deer descend, ducks and songbirds migrate; their roads are flyways, game trails. So, the hunters follow.

The quality of transience is different from spring. A restlessness, nesting, gathering of nuts. Firewood cutting, meat jerking, canning and preserving. Putting on storm windows. Calling your children to hunker.

The RV crowd heads south in pursuit of summer, most of them in the autumn of their lives. The seasonals change jobs: raft guide to school bus driver, trout bum to ski bum. The working migrants follow the onions, then the potatoes, then the apples.

When John Fielder was shooting these stunning photographs, I was driving around Colorado on paths half-covered with yellow leaves. The car would blow through a grove and I'd look back as gold flecks swirled. Looking back is something I do in autumn.

Four boys play football in a late afternoon yard, leaves flying, noses running, their coats thrown down by the edge of a dying garden. I hear a chain saw running, see a pickup half full of aspen, the good feeling of something accomplished. After, the taste of cocoa by a fire. I see a walk with a woman in leaves, a kiss so tender it hurts to separate. Every October her memory returns. Fall is the time to lose a lover.

Autumn bombards the senses and psyche. Choose any picture. See the light. There are physical reasons for the warmth. The sun angle, the reds and yellows, shadows that give the landscape texture. Still, it is more feel than image, mood over reason.

Watch the various stages: rich green swaths, slow drifts of color, patches of stark empty trunks, as if scarred by fire. Then whole hillsides black and white. Skeletons. Fall is a glorious flameout.

In spring we move toward life and bounty. In autumn the road leads to death. We don't like to acknowledge that. We are surprised by the first freeze. We ignore the succession of flowers that tell us the march has begun. We close our eyes to the change in light until, suddenly, the geese go honking.

Autumn is yang and yin, the season that never becomes. Warm days, cold nights, the contrast of snow and grass. The harmony of opposites. That is how we best see, in polarity, life and death — the dualism by which we understand.

Rituals help: Thanksgiving, county fairs, the corn dance. The late Stuart Mace taught me to lie in an aspen grove and look up. There in God's cathedral you can see the end of life with grace. Seeing in the yellow the dying of the green. "As long as you have done your living right, dying in autumn is all right."

Along a country road I drive slowly, watching winter descending through a rear-facing window. The wheat is covered. Moles are burrowed. Bears slumber in their dens. Toward the darkest night I drive.

But in the decay of autumn's leaves the seeds of nature's sowing lie. This is the time for faith, my friend. With autumn's end it is not death you see, but life beginning.

— Jim Carrier
Denver, Colorado

In an aspen forest, Kebler Pass, near Crested Butte

PREFACE

Over the past twenty years, I have been fortunate to experience many beautiful Colorado autumns. Although easterners sometimes deplore our lack of "reds" in the fall palette of turning leaves, the yellows, oranges, and sometimes reds of aspen, and the yellows and oranges of cottonwood trees are more than enough color for me. On top of those, the glorious backlighted reds of the scrub oak provide "icing on the cake."

Autumn of 1993 was the most beautiful I have ever seen. The images within this book are substantially from this time, although I have included photographs from other years. Something happened that year that I had not witnessed before: the scrub oak thickets turned red at the same time the aspens and cottonwoods went yellow! Typically these events are separated by a week or more. What a treat to have reds, oranges, yellows, and greens of the foliage combine with Indian summer blue skies. For photographers and viewers alike, autumn of 1993 was heaven!

After a year of hiking and skiing with a backpack in order to photograph Colorado's other three seasons, autumn is a welcome relief! Most of Colorado's deciduous forests are located below 11,000 feet, and most of that zone is coursed with very scenic roads. So an autumn photography tour doesn't require the leg strength of summer — one can drive to the best places.

I suppose I have driven practically all the dirt and gravel roads of Colorado and have come to learn the location of Colorado's most alluring aspen tree forests. If you've not smelled the sweet fragrance of decaying leaves, or heard their rustling in gentle autumn breezes, you owe yourself a September visit to an aspen forest. And as a bonus, your drives along Colorado's numerous rivers and creeks will provide you views of thick groves of cottonwood trees.

To help you find some of Colorado's most spectacular aspen forests, I have included travel directions in the back of this book. In addition, I have suggested a few ways to improve your own autumn photography. I hope these ideas prove useful to you.

As you travel with me through Colorado in this book, you will be able to experience autumn as it has been expressed by a few very special writers. Between my images and their thoughts I think your love of this glorious time of year will be renewed. At the very least, I sincerely hope that your respect for Colorado's natural environment will be enhanced.

— John Fielder
Englewood, Colorado

Autumn at the Great Sand Dunes National Monument

Other books by John Fielder:

Rocky Mountain National Park: A 100 Year Perspective
To Walk in Wilderness: A Colorado Rocky Mountain Journal
Colorado, Rivers of the Rockies
Along the Colorado Trail
Colorado, Lost Places and Forgotten Words
Colorado Waterfalls Littlebook
Colorado Aspen Trees Littlebook
Colorado Lakes & Creeks Littlebook
Colorado Wildflowers Littlebook
Colorado Reflections Littlebook
The Complete Guide to Colorado Wilderness Areas
Colorado BLM Wildlands: A Guide to Hiking &
    Floating Colorado's Canyon Country

Also look for John Fielder's Colorado wall and engagement calendars.

John Fielder's images are available as fine art prints and stock photography. For information about prints, books, or calendars contact Westcliffe Publishers at (303) 935-0900.

"In spite of autumn's disposal of much of its greenery, there were still, aside from the coniferous trees which seemed much brighter than they had been all summer, a good many leaves in these woods which would remain green all winter....

The very presence of the unfading greenery, the falling away of golden leaves, the color itself, the perfume, all provoked questions which I had a hard time trying to explain. I could perhaps comprehend some of the chemist's explanations — for autumn indeed is a vast chemical laboratory — but the intricate reasons behind the explanations are not so easily understood."

— Virginia Eifert, *Journeys in Green Places*

Mt. Sneffels as seen from Dallas Divide, San Juan Mountains
Pre-dawn light, Dunkley Pass, Routt National Forest

"Since the first deciduous tree rose above the primeval ooze, since birds and beasts first peopled the woodland, there has been this season of leaf-fall and abundance. When man came along, in the slow sequence of evolution, here was October, his for the taking. And over the centuries and the ages, man has made Autumn his own as far as he can ever make any season his own . . . .

If ever there was a season for man to savor this earth and know it intimately, October is its peak and prime.

Winds forever blow, rivers forever run, birds forever fly. But one doesn't have to look to know that now ducks are on the wing, and grouse and pheasants. Bucks are in the thicket. Bears fatten. Fox stalks rabbit, and rabbit is free and whimsical as the wind. Harvests are in, the hasty time is at an end, the whine and bite of Winter are still in the distance, over the hill, beyond the horizon."

— Hal Borland, *This Hill, This Valley*

Sunset on Ragged Peak, McClure Pass, near Redstone
Deep Creek Mesa, near Telluride

"How silent are the woods when the air is still; how filled with sighs and murmurs when a slight breeze springs up; how echoing with the boom and shriek and wail of the treetops when a great wind blows! On this day of tumultuous gusts, the buffeted trees respond to the wind like a vast orchestra of aeolian harps. In a thousand variations, the twigs, the branches, the individual forms of the bare treetops contribute different strains, different tones to the roaring medley that rises and falls around us."

— Edwin Way Teale, *A Walk Through the Year*

Post-sunset light, Kebler Pass, near Crested Butte
Previous Photograph: *Colorado "palms," Dunkley Pass, near Oak Creek*

"I am forty, I have become mortal. I have no further psychic, emotional, or intellectual need to prolong summer seasons, and it is only when autumn begins its play that I can truly focus on the rich and vital life I am living. All of a sudden I grow alert."

— John Nichols, *The Last Beautiful Days of Autumn*

Scrub oak and aspen, Owl Creek Pass, near Ridgway

"The plants of summer, now dead and dry, mingle in their varied shades of yellow and brown — russet and chocolate and tan. I wander aimlessly this way and that, recognizing plants that I stopped beside when they were green, when they were in bloom and visited by bees, when they were just commencing the development of their seeds. All are crisp and brittle. Each plant has completed the beginning, the middle, and the end of its annual life.

In walking among the plants, I am sometimes tempted to view with a tinging of envy the simplicity of their lives. Without straining, without aspiring to more than they can achieve, they grow and bloom and form their seed. The calmness of the plants seems the embodiment of a timeless confidence."

— Edwin Way Teale, *A Walk Through The Year*

Ferns and aspen trees, Routt National Forest,
near Steamboat Springs
Beaver pond, Lime Creek Road, near Purgatory

"Even as the Autumn days shorten they increase in height and breadth. It is as though there were a constant ratio which keeps the days in balance. The leaves are thinning out. The eye can reach. New vistas open....

The hills are no longer remote, and at night I can look up from almost anywhere and see the constellations of Andromeda and Pegasus. Even in a land of trees, we are no longer canopied from the sky or walled in from the horizon. The earth's distances invite the eye. And as the eye reaches, so must the mind stretch to meet these new horizons."

— Hal Borland, *This Hill, This Valley*

Lookout Mountain, Rio Grande National Forest, near Platoro
Fence of aspen boles, Dallas Divide, near Ridgway

"The brilliant autumnal colors are red and yellow and the various tints, hues, and shades of these. Blue is reserved to be the color of the sky, but yellow and red are the colors of the earth-flower. Every fruit, on ripening, and just before its fall, acquires a bright tint. So do the leaves; so the sky before the end of the day, and the year near its setting. October is the red sunset sky, November the later twilight. Color stands for all ripeness and success."

— Henry David Thoreau, *Journal*

A "family" of aspen pinks, Routt National Forest, near Oak Creek
Sunset above Elk Mountain, Routt National Forest, near Steamboat Springs

"October is the month when summer trees become autumn trees and autumn trees become winter trees.... During the nearly six months of our winter trees, the songs of the summer birds and the music of the insects will be replaced by the varied sounds — low or loud, crooning or shrieking — that make up the music of the wind among the leafless twigs and branches.

A chill rain sweeps over us this morning hastening the descent of the remaining leaves. Wherever we go through the dripping woods today, walking on the soggy carpet of fallen foliage, the air is filled with the primal, deeply moving odor of wet autumn leaves, of tissue — alive so short a time ago — beginning its slow process of oxidation and decay, its transformation into woodland mold.

Leaf-fall, in these October days, represents one of the major landmarks of the year. It marks the end of the time of growth, the end — for the deciduous trees — of chlorophyll-making, the end of the green months, the coming of the great change to the predominantly gray and white months. On the wet woodland trails of this day, we have the feeling of walking a ridgetop between the seasons."

— Edwin Way Teale, *A Walk Through the Year*

Dunkley Pass, Routt National Forest, near Oak Creek
At day's end, Uncompahgre National Forest,
near Ridgway

"But in October what a feast to the eye our woods and groves present! The whole body of the air seems enriched by their calm, slow radiance. They are giving back the light they have been absorbing from the sun all summer."

— John Burroughs, *John Burroughs' America*

Sunrise and Pyramid Peak, Routt National Forest
The Dyke stands behind aspen groves along the Kebler Pass road, near Crested Butte
Previous Photograph: *Pastures near Ridgway*

"The hints of approaching fall are on every hand. How suggestive this thistledown…which, as I sit by the open window, comes in and brushes softly across my hand! The first snowflake tells of winter not more plainly than this driving down heralds the approach of fall."

— John Burroughs, *John Burroughs' America*

Uncompahgre National Forest, near Ridgway
Autumn snows, Weston Pass, near Fairplay

"Several hours after the earlier dusk of this last November day, we watch the rising of the moon. We see it lift, disengage itself from the maze of the silhouetted treetops, then mount, in slow motion, up the seeming curve of the cloudless sky. This November moon, only a few days past full, the beaver moon of the Indians, is pale, cold silver. Its shining disk is almost as round, almost as large as that of the harvest moon of earlier fall. But gone is the warmth, gone the golden light that lengthened the days for pioneers working in their fields.

Our way lit by this colder moonlight, we walk in the night. We see its pale rays glinting on the new ice of the pond. We see its silver light spreading across the frost mantle of the meadows. Everything there is glowing and silvered — double silver, the silver moonlight on the silver frost. We breathe in the air, cold and pure. We stop now and then to look up at the stars, paler stars in the moonlit sky. But when we stop beneath our... trees and catch the light of the stars among their branches, they shine with their old brilliance. Here, where our eyes are shaded from the dominant light of the moon, we see the glitter of pin-point lights enmeshed in the treetops, the stars and the contorted, leafless limbs intermingling."

— Edwin Way Teale, *A Walk Through the Year*

Post-sunset light, Dunkley Pass, Routt National Forest

"There is a chill in it and an exhilaration also. The forenoon is all morning and the afternoon all evening. The shadows seem to come forth and to revenge themselves upon the day. The sunlight is diluted with darkness. The colors fade from the landscape, and only the sheen of the river lights up the gray and brown distance."

— John Burroughs, *John Burroughs' America*

Cottonwood trees along Ohio Creek, near Gunnison

"The time of the falling of leaves has come again. Once more in our morning walk we tread upon carpets of gold and crimson, of brown and bronze....

How beautifully the leaves grow old! How full of light and color are their last days!"

— John Burroughs, *John Burroughs' America*

Black Mesa, along State Highway 92, near Blue Mesa Reservoir

"...autumn will always in some way be associated with the Indian.... The smoke of his campfire seems again in the air. The memory of him pervades the woods.... The time of the chase, the season of the buck and the doe and of the ripening of all forest fruits; the time when all men are incipient hunters, when the first frosts have given pungency to the air, when to be abroad on the hills or in the woods is a delight that both old and young feel..."

— John Burroughs, *John Burroughs' America*

September frost, Kebler Pass, near Crested Butte
After the storm, Castle Pines, near Denver

"Every few years the clean blue autumn has a trick of enduring almost beyond belief. One incredibly clear day follows another, through October, into November, occasionally into December.... And the high country lingers in exquisite languid suspension. The preposterous soul-stirring arrogance of aspen-yellow hillsides flames brightly..."

— John Nichols, *The Last Beautiful Days of Autumn*

Moonrise, Routt National Forest, near Oak Creek
Sunrise in the Routt National Forest
Previous Photograph: *Along the Elk River, near Steamboat Springs*

"There is an old notion that autumn is a melancholy time best suited to dirges and sad laments. Bryant wrote of its days as 'the saddest of the year.' But I know of few places on this continent where autumn fails to provide some of the most beautiful days of the year. The dust of summer has begun to settle, first hard frost clears the air, and October skies can be as clear and blue as a baby's eyes. Even Indian Summer, with its haze and its misty dawns, has a special lure."

— Hal Borland, *Homeland, A Report from the Country*

"Red" aspen trees, Spring Creek Pass, San Juan Mountains
Conejos Peak, above Platoro Reservoir, Rio Grande National Forest

"I accept autumn as a ritual of celebration. All life is heightened and precious; all anguish is bittersweet, unfailingly real.... And I have no fear of winter."

— John Nichols, *The Last Beautiful Days of Autumn*

McClure Pass, near Redstone

"Autumn ebbs away into winter, but there is flow rather than ebb in the unseen wind tides that now lap at the hills and send their invisible breakers to hiss softly in the upper woodlands. They are the tides that curl about this earth, forever restless and eternally moving, tides that obey some subtler master than the moon."

— Hal Borland, *This Hill, This Valley*

Solitary aspen, on the Crystal River, near Redstone

"Already, as I go down the lane this morning, my feet scuff through the initial layer of the fallen ash leaves. Here and there I am surrounded by the leisurely drift of spent foliage descending in the only journey of its life from the twigs of the ash trees to the lane below. The slender leaves are like the first deliberate flakes of a snowstorm.

And when I go to the woods in the afternoon, I notice already a perceptible increase in the widening of my view. New vistas are opening up. Secret places are revealed. In this bush I glimpse the nest where a brood was raised unobserved. On that tree limb I see another nest that has been screened by leaves before. The mystery of where birds we met a hundred times along these trails cared for their young becomes, with even a slight thinning of the clothing of the trees, a mystery no longer. Like the opening pages of a book, the woodland scene is spreading out. From now on, as we go along these paths, we will learn progressively something new about something old as we see revealed what the dense foliage of summer has hidden before."

— Edwin Way Teale, *A Walk Through the Year*

The aspen bole fence, Dallas Divide, San Juan Mountains
Old road in the Routt National Forest,
near Steamboat Springs

"It is, say, the last of October or the first of November. The air is not balmy, but tart and pungent, like the flavor of the red-cheeked apples by the roadside. In the sky not a cloud, not a speck; a vast dome of blue ether lightly suspended above the world. The woods are heaped with color like a painter's palette — great splashes of red and orange and gold.... In the glens and nooks it is so still that the chirp of a solitary cricket is noticeable."

—John Burroughs, *John Burroughs' America*

Aspen trees and grass, Black Mesa, above Blue Mesa Reservoir
Sunset, Routt National Forest, near Steamboat Springs
Previous Photograph: *Last leaves of autumn, above Castle Creek, near Aspen*

"Autumn on the clearing is the realization of death, which is only a quickened sense of life. The feeling of quiet hurry, of transition, of an erratic but nonetheless fated drift toward winter, is pervasive — sundown each day comes earlier; each morning the green . . . has given further way to the seeping invasion of deadly color, each day when the deer come to the apple trees, the steel blue hair of their winter coats is more pronounced; the black cat, which all summer has shunned humanity, comes with increasing regularity to the kitchen; each day there is a larger build-up of ducks on the marshes."

— Hugh Fosburgh, *A Clearing in the Wilderness*

Marcelina Mountain, along the Kebler Pass road, near Crested Butte
Old cabin, along the Cimarron River, Uncompahgre National Forest

"I live for autumn. All year long I have reveries of those cool beautiful days to come, and memories of Octobers past. It is the most alive, the most heartbreakingly real season in my bones. I love the chilly winds and dying leaves and the first snow flurries that sweep intermittently down this lean valley."

— John Nichols, *The Last Beautiful Days of Autumn*

Approaching storm, Weston Pass, near Fairplay
Indian summer blue skies, along the Yampa River,
near Steamboat Springs

"In another month of October, on just such a day as this, the Swiss philosopher, Henri Amiel, wrote in his *Journal Intime:* 'One feels the hours gently slipping by, and time, instead of flying, seems to hover.'

This sense of time standing still, of hours lengthening, of a slower ticking of the clock — this mood of the lingering days that is peculiar to October — is everywhere around us as we advance, in sunshine and shadow, along our trails today. All is warm and still. Winter seems far away. The insects of the meadow sing on as though they would sing forever. This is the plateau before the mountain climb, the still pool before the rapids, the lull before the storm. It is a time rich in beauty before a time of bleakness. It is a drifting time before the great reversal.

I know that once in May I chose those days of spring as the finest of the year. And I may think so again when I am in the midst of another spring. But now it seems to me it is these few lingering days of October that must be the finest of all. In them, as in the days of spring, there is beauty, sunshine, genial conditions. But here there is an added quality, a sense of maturity, of having experienced more, a greater sense of knowing, a sense of ripening, of fulfillment, of acceptance. October is the culmination of the alterations of the year. This happiness, this deep content, that comes in the serenity of these few latter days, is based on all that has gone before, is heightened by the proximity to change."

— Edwin Way Teale, *A Walk Through the Year*

Last Dollar Road, near Telluride

"The pace changes. It is not exactly a time for leisure, but there is occasion now to look at the far hills and think thoughts not bounded by a cornstalk's height or a pasture's breadth. The big rhythms seep into the soul, the rhythms of the seasons and the years rather than the rhythms of long days and short nights....

Autumn is for understanding, for the longer thoughts and the deeper comprehensions. How well it is that the year should bring such a time, to rest the muscles, yes, from the Summer's tensions, but even more important to relax the mind and give it time to span the valleys of belief. Now a man's mind can reach beyond himself."

—Hal Borland, *This Hill, This Valley*

Evening light colors pine and scrub oak, Castle Pines, near Denver

"When I go out of an evening now and see the Big Dipper down on the northern horizon I know that it is pointing the time of all time, just as the clock of the stars has been doing since they were patterned in the night sky. The grass still grows, the oats ripen, the leaves fall, the frosts still come, and winter blows its snowy gales on the same schedule they had before my kind was here to know them. If I abide by that schedule I can manage to live in relative comfort, but the minute I forget it or ignore it, I am courting trouble, and neither clocks nor computers can save me."

— Hal Borland, *Homeland, A Report from the Country*

Autumn snows, along East Dallas Creek, Sneffels Range

"We walked in so pure and bright a light, gilding the withered grass and leaves, so softly and serenely bright, I thought I had never bathed in such a golden flood, without a ripple or a murmur to it. The west side of every wood and rising ground gleamed like the boundary of Elysium, and the sun on our backs seemed like a gentle herdsman driving us home at evening.

So we saunter toward the Holy Land, till one day the sun shall shine more brightly than ever he has done, shall perchance shine into our minds and hearts, and light up our whole lives with a great awakening light, as warm and serene and golden as on a bankside in autumn."

— Henry David Thoreau, *Autumn in New England*

Driving through the aspen forest, near Ridgway
Cimarron Ridge, Uncompahgre National Forest,
near Ridgway

"Everybody should own a tree at this time of year. Or a valley full of trees, or a whole hillside. Not legally, in the formal 'Know all men' way, written on a piece of paper, but in the way that one comes to own a tree by seeing it at the turn of the road, or down the street, or in a park, and watching it day after day and seeing color come to its leaves. That way it is your tree forever, any time you choose to pass that way, and neither fence nor title can take it from you."

— Hal Borland, *This Hill, This Valley*

Clearing storm, along the Conejos River, Rio Grande National Forest
Mt. Sneffels, San Juan Mountains, near Ridgway
Previous Photograph: *Along the Alamosa River, Rio Grande National Forest*

"The morning was filled with a stirring fragrance. It was late autumn...mid-October — and most of the leaves had fallen; yet their perfume remained more potently strong than ever....Cold, wind, and rain had whipped off the leaves like bright flags and had flung them on the ground where, somewhat muted yet still colorful, they lay in a multihued carpet....

Late autumn brought a distinctly different set of values and a new means of rating a landscape which was heading into the winter. It was revelatory and delightful. It was as if the autumn's changes had opened a door to new vistas which I had found no way to unlatch before. I could find no mournfulness here, no regret for lost leaves and flowers and buds. All about me were the living promises of next year's leaves and blossoms. They were packaged small and well-enwrapped for safest keeping."

— Virginia Eifert, *Journeys in Green Places*

Hillside of color, Beaver Creek Wilderness Study Area,
near Colorado Springs
Early snows, Mt. Sneffels Wilderness, near Ridgway

"The fall of '74 was the most remarkable...I remember ever to have seen. The equilibrium of the season lasted from the middle of October till near December, with scarcely a break. There were six weeks of Indian summer, all gold by day, and, when the moon came, all silver by night. The river was so smooth at times as to be almost invisible, and in its place was the indefinite continuation of the opposite shore down toward the nether world. One seemed to be in an enchanted land, and to breathe all day the atmosphere of fable and romance. Not a smoke, but a kind of shining nimbus filled all the spaces. The vessels would drift by as if in mid-air with all their sails set. The gypsy blood in one, as Lowell calls it, could hardly stay between four walls and see such days go by. Living in tents, in groves and on the hills, seemed the only natural life."

— John Burroughs, *Great Wilderness Days*

Looking towards the Flat Tops Wilderness,
from Dunkley Pass, near Oak Creek
Cottonwood trees along the Dolores River, near Dolores

"I watched a crow go winging past this morning and he looked twice as black as he did two months ago. But it was the same crow, or at least one of the same flock, that has been here all year. Maybe its plumage is new, but it is the same color. The difference is in the background, which is now gray and brown and slightly misty today. The crow is no blacker, but he looks so in this new setting. When the snow comes, he will look blacker still. . . .

Color becomes relative as the seasons shift. Brilliance is less a matter of color itself than one of contrast. The less there is to see, the more one sees of it. The eyes sharpen as the days turn chill and the woods turn gray."

— Hal Borland, *This Hill, This Valley*

Along the Engineer Pass road, near Lake City

"We speak of the wind and its voices, but most of the voices are in the trees. And even those voices vary from season to season, almost from month to month. . . .

Aspens and cottonwoods whisper in anything but an absolute calm; give them a breeze and you can hear them afar, fairly chattering, their heart-shaped leaves on long, limber stems, each leaf dancing against a dozen others. . . .

The evergreens, the pines and spruces. . . . hum rather than speak, and theirs is closest of all to music. The music of the pines is heard best at night, and best of all on a Winter night when their deciduous brothers of the woodland stand stark in the starlight."

— Hal Borland, *This Hill, This Valley*

The Beckwith Mountains, along the Kebler Pass road, near Crested Butte

JOHN FIELDER'S COLORADO

A Great Northern Colorado Autumn Auto Tour

One place in particular I love returning to time and again is the Trappers Lake portion of the White River and Routt National Forests. Southwest of the town of Steamboat Springs, this land of rolling hills and flat-topped mountains contains vast groves of aspen on the hillsides and stately cottonwood trees in the river and creek bottoms.

There is an extensive network of county-maintained gravel roads penetrating all but the most remote of these forests. These roads are not maintained in winter, but spring, summer and fall they are a delight to drive. And getting there takes one along highways boasting their own displays of autumn gold!

Find your way to the town of Wolcott 20 miles west of Vail on I-70. Go north on State Highway 131 about 49 miles to the town of Phippsburg. Just before Phippsburg head southwest on County Road 15, which takes you to National Forest Road 16 and over Dunkley Pass. From here on, you will witness some of Colorado's most spectacular displays of aspen trees.

Northern Colorado aspen groves turn color sooner than in other parts of the state. Greens begin turning to gold in early September, and trees can lose their leaves as early as the third week of the month. Typically, though, best color here is from September 15 to 25.

Continue your drive down to the East Fork Williams Fork River. Proceed south to Vaughn Lake and down to the White River. Here you head west to Trappers Lake, one of Colorado's most beautiful, surrounded by the cliffs of the Flat Tops Wilderness.

Go home the same way you came, or follow the East Fork Williams Fork northwest on a circuitous, yet scenic drive to the town of Hamilton on State Highway 13. There are numerous other well-maintained roads in this neck of the woods, but be sure to take along the Routt National Forest map. Plan on a weekend trip, and at least a full day in the forest.

There is no better time to take a hike than on a 65 degree, dry September afternoon. There are numerous trails that take off from the roads along which you will be driving. Most are quite easy and you will find that only a short hike away from the road will reveal new sights, sounds, and smells. There are several especially scenic, though relatively steep, trails leaving the Trappers Lake area for the surrounding wilderness.

A Great Southern Colorado Autumn Auto Tour

I've discovered that the aspen groves of southwest Colorado assume their autumn posture about a week later than the rest of the state. Some years they won't lose their leaves until the second week of October.

More often than not, though, the best viewing of fall color in the Ouray-Ridgway-Telluride corridor is September 25 to October 5. So if you've missed the chance to visit the mountains in September, all may not be lost!

One of my favorite aspen viewing routes that takes advantage of improved county roads is the Owl Creek Pass drive. Along the way you will witness the incredibly colorful combination of the fire-reds of scrub oak and the golds of aspen. As a bonus, you will see some of Colorado's most serrated and craggy peaks all around you.

Previous Photograph: *An autumn sunset from Owl Creek Pass, near Ridgway*

The town of Ridgway is 26 miles south of Montrose. About three miles north of Ridgway on US Highway 550 turn east on County Road 10. Views across lush pastures towards the surrounding peaks of the Mt. Sneffels and Uncompahgre Wilderness Areas will astound you. Massive cottonwoods will be changing color, just like the aspens higher up.

County Road 10 soon meets National Forest Road 858, which winds its way up to Owl Creek Pass at elevation 11,120 feet. Views of Courthouse Mountain to the south, and Mt. Sneffels to the southwest are simply awe inspiring. Here at the Pass there are several trails that do not require much penetration to appreciate the subalpine environment. Make sure to take with you, for both road and trail routing, the Uncompahgre National Forest map.

At Owl Creek Pass, the road heads north down the West Fork of the Cimarron River. You will pass through more spectacular aspen groves and eventually pass by Silver Jack Reservoir, a popular fishing spot! For the next 20 miles you will cross through beautiful ranching country on your way to a rendezvous with US Highway 50 about 35 miles west of Montrose. Plan on spending at least half a day on this route.

This trip can be done as a one-way excursion as described, or you can turn around at the top of the pass and go back to Ridgway. If you make the trip to Highway 50, at that point you are only 18 miles from the entrance to Black Canyon of the Gunnison National Monument. Why not visit Colorado's narrowest and deepest canyon?

If you end up in the Ridgway area, you may want to consider spending a night in Telluride, about an hour away. The aspen groves on that side of the mountain are unique unto themselves.

How To Photograph Aspen Trees — A Few Tips

Light

Time of day determines just how golden those aspen trees will appear on film. Nevertheless, this great tree in its autumn state does not have a "bad side," for under any light they are spectacular.

If you want to photograph the true golds of autumn, you need the low lying sun of morning or evening. Photograph into the sun, so that the leaves are back lighted. Because they are translucent, the sunlight shines through, causing them to glow in shades of gold. But be careful not to let the sun shine directly into your lens. That will cause hexagonal lens flares on the film. Try to block the sun with the trunk of a tree.

As much as I enjoy photographing back-lighted aspens, I also enjoy the subtle yellows in cloudy light. White clouds in the sky, but not dark gray storm clouds, will reflect a soft white light onto the leaves. This is a great time to make closeup images of the leaves fallen to the ground or still on branches. In addition, the white trunks of the aspen will not be so "hot" or overexposed, as they are in direct sunlight.

The Tree

Without a doubt, my favorite tree is the aspen. From one season to the next, its character changes more than any other one I know. Each season makes for great photographs. In winter, there are no leaves, so one's eyes go quickly to those linear, parallel trunks, or boles. From white to gray to green, they come in all shades. But no matter the color or season, a telephoto lens aimed at a grove from some distance away will emphasize their unique symmetry and straightness.

Put on a wide-angle lens and stand beneath the trees within a grove. Aim your camera up about 30 degrees and watch the parallel trunks diverge and lose parallax. Golden leaves silhouetted against a clear blue sky are startling in their intensity. Now aim the camera, with either a standard or wide-angle lens, straight up to the sky. If you're standing in a dense grove, you can make a picture of leaves and tree tops that form a circular ring against the sky. Spectacular!

"Long ago, I suppose, the autumns must have been a good deal more simple to know and to explain than they are today....Today, in order to explain autumn and to understand only some of its marvels, I have to know something of plant anatomy and biochemistry, which are maybe not as romantic, but are inconceivably more fascinating. Each explanation of something hitherto unknown, or long ignored, opens for me another door to a wider wonder of the world....

Yet, in finding partial answers for these questions, I always come upon more which are still unexplained. It would be a pity if they were all answered and there were no more questions, no more queries, no more inexplicable wonders. Knowledge is good, but wonder is priceless. The one is of the mind, the other of the spirit."

— Virginia Eifert, *Journeys in Green Places*

Along the Conejos River, Rio Grande National Forest